T0004652

West Coast
ABCs

Jocey Asnong

RMB

Boats float
under bridges

British Columbia

B

Cathedral Grove

Climb
the
tallest
cedar
tree

Dolphins
dive in
the sea

Departure Bay

Elk Falls

Eagle eyes watch fish fly

H

G

Glide down groomed hills

Grouse Mountain

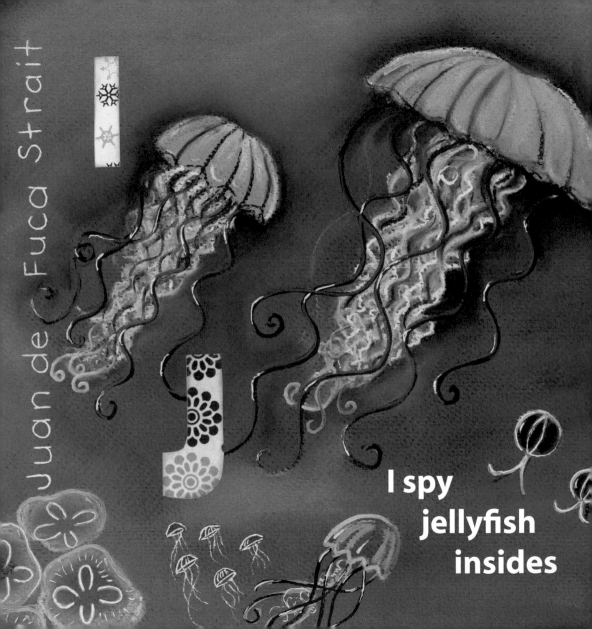

Juan de Fuca Strait

J j

I spy
jellyfish
insides

K

Let's kayak to a lighthouse

L

Langara Island

Mermaids make seaweed braids

Mayne Island

M

Octopus Islands

Orca
plays with
octopus

Paddle past porpoises

Qualicum Beach

**Quail
squawks
as she
walks**

Raven soars over rainforest

R

Refugium Range

**Seal surfs
in the sun**

South Chesterman Beach

Tides bring treasures

Telegraph Cove

Put up our
umbrellas

**Voles visit
flower gardens**

Victoria

We watch
for whale
tails

Wickaninnish Beach

It's exciting
to explore

Expo Centre

Young
wolf yawns
goodnight

Yakoun River

Zodiac zips us to our island home

Zeballos Inlet

Copyright © 2022 by Jocey Asnong

All rights reserved. No part of this publication may be reproduced, stored in a retrieval system, or transmitted in any form or by any means – electronic, mechanical, audio recording, or otherwise – without the written permission of the publisher or a photocopying licence from Access Copyright. Permissions and licensing contribute to a secure and vibrant book industry by helping to support writers and publishers through the purchase of authorized editions and excerpts. To obtain an official licence, please visit accesscopyright.ca or call 1-800-893-5777.

RMB | Rocky Mountain Books Ltd.
rmbooks.com
@rmbooks
facebook.com/rmbooks

Cataloguing data available from Library and Archives Canada
ISBN 9781771605038 (pbk.)

Design by Chyla Cardinal

Printed and bound in China by 1010 Printing International Ltd.

Distributed in Canada by Heritage Group Distribution and in the U.S. by Publishers Group West

For information on purchasing bulk quantities of this book, or to obtain media excerpts or invite the author to speak at an event, please visit rmbooks.com and select the "Contact Us" tab.

RMB | Rocky Mountain Books is dedicated to the environment and committed to reducing the destruction of old-growth forests. Our books are produced with respect for the future and consideration for the past.

We acknowledge the financial support of the Government of Canada through the Canada Book Fund and the Canada Council for the Arts, and of the province of British Columbia through the British Columbia Arts Council and the Book Publishing Tax Credit.

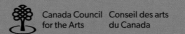
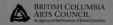